# PATHWAYS

USING A WIOA YOUTH PROGRAM TO GET FREE
TUITION FOR COLLEGE AND CAREER TRAINING

MARQUES J. CLARK

This book is designed to provide information that the author believes to be accurate on the subject matter it covers, but it is sold with the understanding that neither the author nor the publisher is offering individualized advice tailored to any individual's specific needs. This book is not intended to articulate the procedures of every WIOA Youth program provider, rather it serves as a best practice for engaging with a WIOA Youth program. This book does not intend to serve as the basis for any financial decision. A professional's services should be utilized if expert assistance is needed.

Pathways: Using a WIOA Youth Program to Get Free Tuition for College and Career Training.

Copyright © 2022 by Marques J. Clark.

All rights reserved. Printed in the United States of America. Aurora, Illinois. No part of this book may be used or reproduced in any manner whatsoever without the prior written permission of the copyright owner except in the case of brief quotations embodied in critical articles and reviews.

Photography by Unsplash.

ISBN: 978-1-7344714-3-4

FIRST EDITION

# TABLE OF CONTENTS

| | |
|---|---|
| 1 | AUTHOR'S NOTE |
| 3 | INTRODUCTION |
| 11 | CHAPTER ONE: WHAT'S A WIOA YOUTH PROGRAM? |
| 31 | CHAPTER TWO: WHO'S ELIGIBLE FOR A WIOA YOUTH PROGRAM? |
| 39 | CHAPTER THREE: HOW DO I APPLY FOR A WIOA YOUTH PROGRAM? |
| 47 | CHAPTER FOUR: HOW DO I FIND BALANCE IN A WIOA YOUTH PROGRAM? |
| 63 | CHAPTER FIVE: WHAT ACADEMIC RESOURCES CAN HELP ME SUCCEED IN A WIOA YOUTH PROGRAM? |
| 79 | CHAPTER SIX: WHAT CAN I DO FOR MY MENTAL HEALTH IN A WIOA YOUTH PROGRAM? |
| 91 | CHAPTER SEVEN: HOW CAN A WIOA YOUTH PROGRAM PREPARE ME FOR MY CAREER? |
| 107 | CHAPTER EIGHT: WHAT'S NEXT AFTER COMPLETING A WIOA YOUTH PROGRAM? |
| 117 | NOTES |
| 119 | ABOUT THE AUTHOR |

# AUTHOR'S NOTE

Pathways was created to spread the word about WIOA (Workforce Innovation and Opportunity Act) Youth programs. This book is not intended to be a comprehensive or exhaustive resource. Instead, Pathways is a lookbook—a visual guide containing photos, graphics, and easy-to-follow actions for using a WIOA Youth program to get free tuition for college and career training.

This book is for anyone interested in the benefits of WIOA Youth programs. WIOA has many programs aimed to help individuals remove barriers to education and employment. This book specifically provides information on "out-of-school" youth programs in WIOA—which the Department of Labor defines as an individual who is between the ages of 16-24, currently out of high school (dropped out or graduated), not yet enrolled in college credit courses, and has an identified barrier to completing education and/or employment.

To get the most out of this book it is recommended that you read it in its entirety. Although, skimming is encouraged, especially if you are looking for something specific. For those who want to jump right in and get started with a WIOA Youth program, below is a QR code that will help you find WIOA Youth providers in your area.

SCAN HERE TO FIND WIOA YOUTH
PROVIDERS IN YOUR AREA

# INTRODUCTION

# The idea of attending college may seem overwhelming.

In fact, the idea of attending college would make anyone's mind start racing—especially if it's your first time attending…

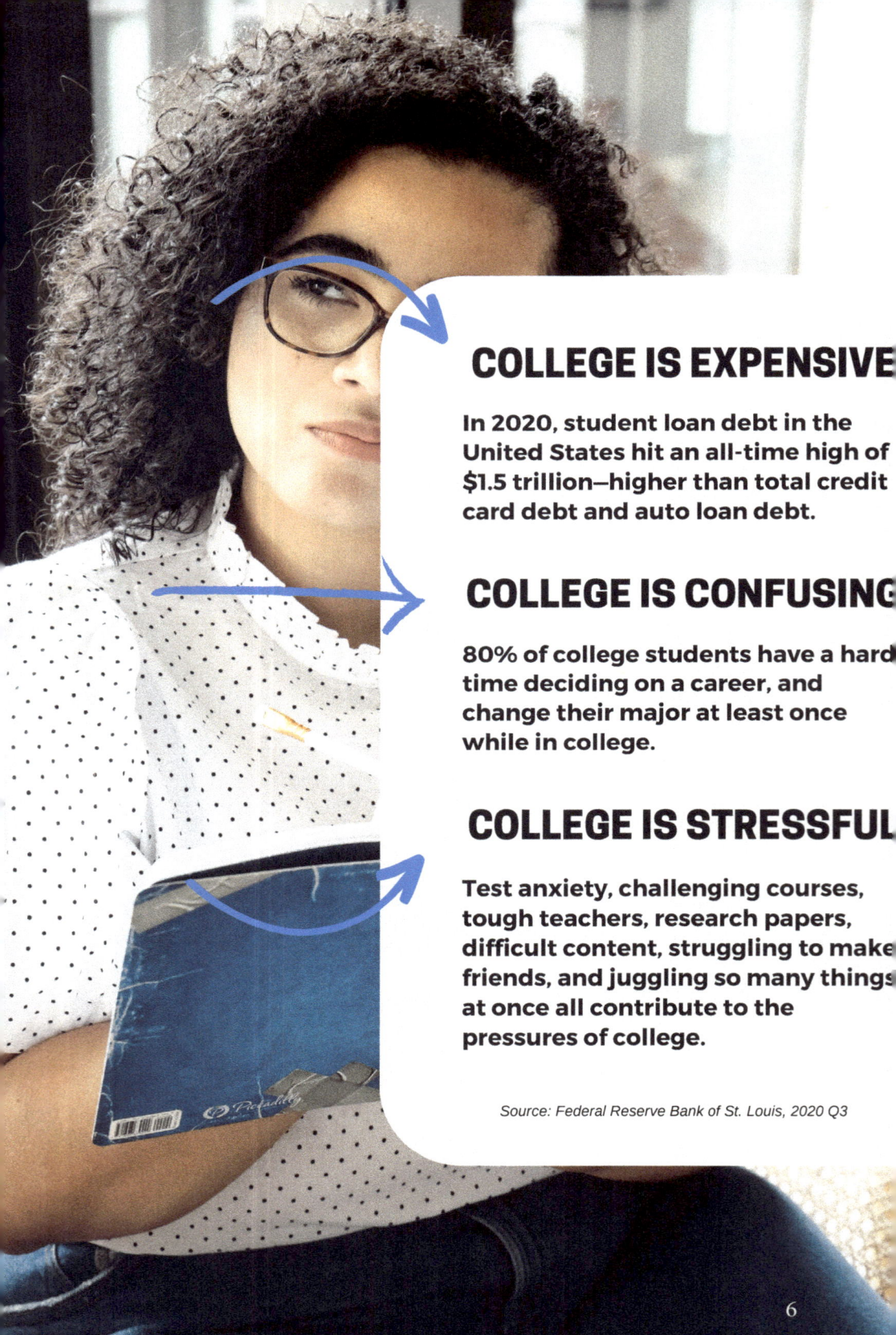

## COLLEGE IS EXPENSIVE

In 2020, student loan debt in the United States hit an all-time high of $1.5 trillion—higher than total credit card debt and auto loan debt.

## COLLEGE IS CONFUSING

80% of college students have a hard time deciding on a career, and change their major at least once while in college.

## COLLEGE IS STRESSFUL

Test anxiety, challenging courses, tough teachers, research papers, difficult content, struggling to make friends, and juggling so many things at once all contribute to the pressures of college.

Source: Federal Reserve Bank of St. Louis, 2020 Q3

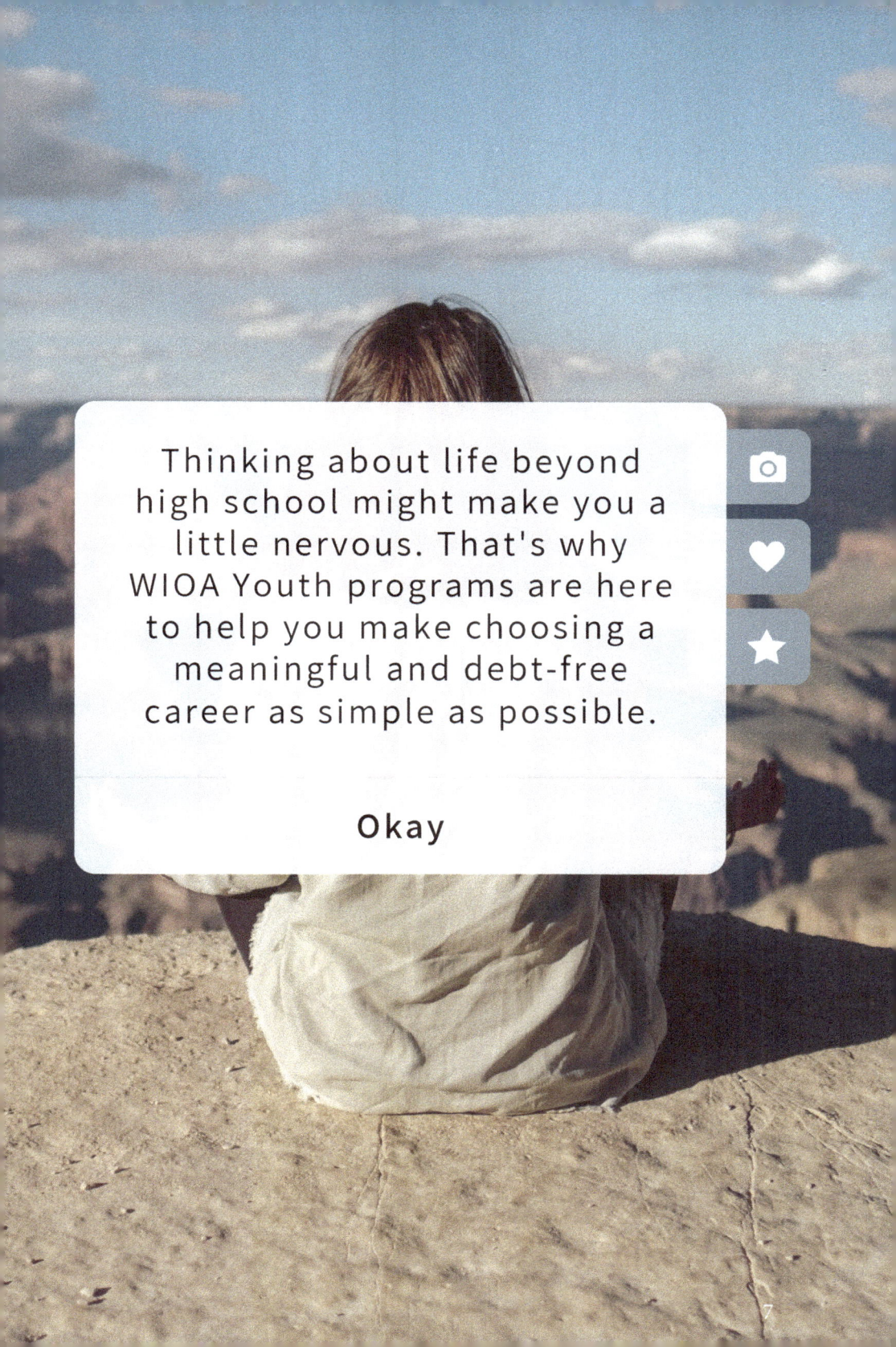

Thinking about life beyond high school might make you a little nervous. That's why WIOA Youth programs are here to help you make choosing a meaningful and debt-free career as simple as possible.

**Okay**

# 30 WAYS A WIOA YOUTH

- TUITION IS FREE
- BOOKS ARE FREE
- YOU CAN PARTICIPATE IN A PAID-WORK EXPERIENCE SUCH AS AN INTERNSHIP
- TRANSPORTATIONS COSTS TO CLASS ARE COVERED
- YOU MEET EMPLOYERS
- YOU CAN WORK WITH A MENTOR
- SCHOOL SUPPLIES ARE FREE
- MEDICAL-RELATED EXPENSES CAN BE COVERED
- YOU CAN JOB SHADOW
- YOU LEARN LIFE SKILLS
- YOU HAVE THE OPTION OF EARNING A CERTIFICATE OR A DEGREE
- YOU RECEIVE HELP WITH ACCOMMODATIONS IF YOU HAVE A DISABILITY
- YOU RECEIVE PRACTICE INTERVIEWING
- COUNSELING/THERAPY EXPENSES ARE COVERED IF YOU NEED THEM
- YOU GET FREE GAS CARDS FOR WORK

# PROGRAM CAN HELP ME

- CHILDCARE COSTS ARE COVERED BY THE PROGRAM
- YOU LEARN FINANCIAL LITERACY
- YOU CAN RECEIVE HELP WITH RENTAL AND HOUSING COSTS
- FREE UBER AND LYFT RIDES
- YOU CAN RECEIVE ASSISTANCE WITH LEGAL FEES
- YOU CAN CHOOSE FROM HUNDREDS OF CAREER PROGRAMS
- YOU CAN RECEIVE A TUTOR
- YOU CAN TOUR BUSINESS FACILITIES
- YOU CAN RECEIVE HELP TRANSFERRING TO A UNIVERSITY
- YOU CAN EARN MORE THAN ONE CREDENTIAL
- YOU CAN RECEIVE HELP STARTING YOUR BUSINESS
- WORK ATTIRE IS COVERED BY THE PROGRAM
- REFERRALS TO JOBS
- YOU CAN RECEIVE A LAPTOP FOR CLASS
- YOU RECEIVE RESUME ASSISTANCE

# CHAPTER ONE:
# WHAT'S A WIOA YOUTH PROGRAM?

# WHAT'S A WIOA YOUTH PROGRAM?

The Workforce Innovation and Opportunity Act (WIOA) is a policy that was created by the U.S. federal government in 2014 to help job-seekers by removing barriers that lead to education and employment. WIOA uses grant funds, distributed to each state by the Department of Labor, to cover expenses for education/training, employment, and supportive services. Through WIOA Youth programs, students can pursue certificates, associate's degrees, bachelor's degrees, and master's degrees. There are hundreds of programs to choose from, and credentials can be obtained from four-year public institutions, for-profit institutions, and community-based organizations.

# IN-SCHOOL VS. OUT-OF-SCHOOL

There are two categories of WIOA Youth programs: In-School Youth and Out-of-School Youth.

**Out-of-School Youth (OSY) are individuals who:**

- completed high school but have not enrolled in college.
- dropped out of high school.
- are not younger than age 16 or older than age 24.

**In-School Youth (ISY) are individuals who:**

- are attending school (high school).
- are not younger than age 14 or older than age 21.
- are of the low-income status according to the Department of Labor.

Both In-School Youth and Out-of-School Youth must also meet basic eligibility requirements in order to be eligible for a WIOA Youth program.

*Pathways specifically focuses on Out-of-School Youth (OSY) when referencing "WIOA Youth programs."*

# WHAT CAN I DO IN A WIOA YOUTH PROGRAM?

## WIOA YOUTH PROGRAM ELEMENTS

WIOA Youth programs have "program elements" or activities that you can participate in during your time in the program. There are a total of 14 program elements in WIOA Youth programs:

**#1** TUTORING, STUDY SKILLS TRAINING, INSTRUCTION, AND DROPOUT PREVENTION

**#2** ALTERNATIVE SECONDARY SCHOOL SERVICES OR DROPOUT RECOVERY SERVICES

**#3** PAID AND UNPAID WORK EXPERIENCE

**#4** OCCUPATIONAL SKILLS TRAINING

**#5** EDUCATION OFFERED CONCURRENTLY WITH WORKFORCE PREPARATION/TRAINING FOR A SPECIFIC OCCUPATION

**#6** PROGRAM LEADERSHIP DEVELOPMENT OPPORTUNITIES

**#7** SUPPORTIVE SERVICES

**#8** ADULT MENTORING

**#9** FOLLOW-UP SERVICES

**#10** COMPREHENSIVE GUIDANCE AND COUNSELING

**#11** FINANCIAL LITERACY EDUCATION

**#12** ENTREPRENEURIAL SKILLS TRAINING

**#13** SERVICES THAT PROVIDE LABOR MARKET INFORMATION

**#14** POST-SECONDARY PREPARATION AND TRANSITION ACTIVITIES

### #1

## TUTORING, STUDY SKILLS TRAINING, INSTRUCTION, AND DROPOUT PREVENTION

WIOA Youth programs provide tools, resources, and strategies to help you identify areas of academic concern, and they help you overcome learning obstacles. These strategies include tutoring, literacy development, active learning experiences, after-school opportunities, individualized instruction, and activities that help prevent a student from dropping out of high school.

## ALTERNATIVE SECONDARY SCHOOL SERVICES OR DROPOUT RECOVERY SERVICES

Alternative secondary school services or dropout recovery services may include basic education skills training, English as a Second Language training, credit recovery, counseling, and many more. Dropout recovery services such as credit recovery, counseling, and educational plan development, are those that can assist you and provide you with options if you have dropped out of school.

# #3

## PAID AND UNPAID WORK EXPERIENCE

---

WIOA Youth programs provide opportunities for you to get paid for the work you perform in a paid-work experience. Paid-work experiences are career opportunities for you to gain skills in your desired job industry. Your paid-work experience can take place in a school, small business, large corporation, or a non-profit organization. Paid-work experiences can last up to 12 weeks and can be in-person or remote. The goal of your paid-work experience is to provide career exploration, skill development, and valuable competencies that will be helpful to secure a permanent employment opportunity in the future. Unpaid work experiences are short-term opportunities that can last a few hours, one day, a week, or more. Examples of unpaid work experiences are job shadowing and structured volunteer work.

# #4

## OCCUPATIONAL SKILLS TRAINING

———————

Occupational Skills Training (or participation in college courses) is one of the most popular program elements because it can cover the cost of tuition and books with grant funds that function like a scholarship. You are not limited to the type of program to choose from either as there are hundreds of options available. You can earn a short-term certificate, advanced certificate, associate's degree, bachelor's degree, and in some cases, even a master's degree. Each program option is designed to assist you in transitioning into the job industry of your choice.

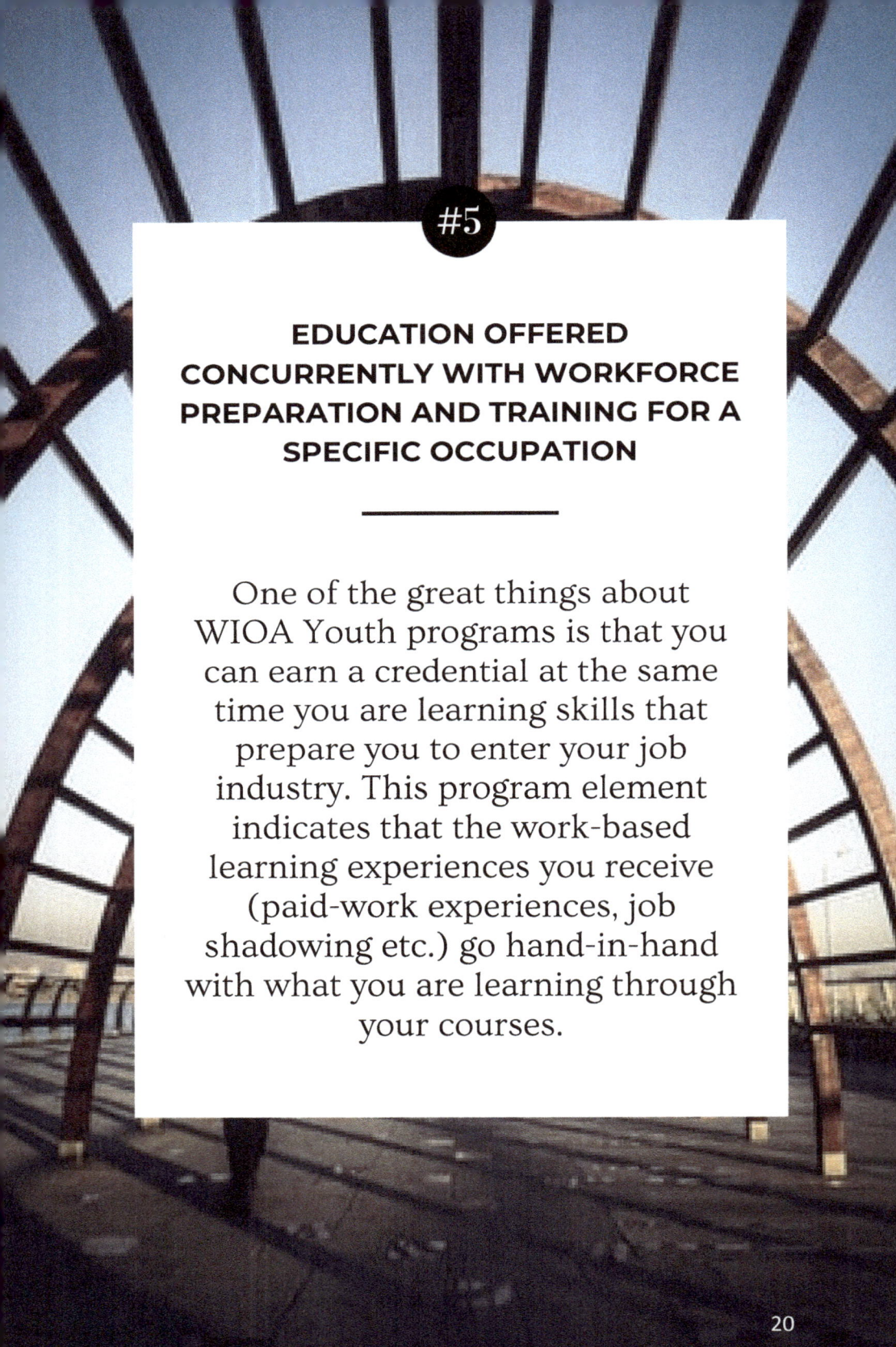

### #5

**EDUCATION OFFERED CONCURRENTLY WITH WORKFORCE PREPARATION AND TRAINING FOR A SPECIFIC OCCUPATION**

One of the great things about WIOA Youth programs is that you can earn a credential at the same time you are learning skills that prepare you to enter your job industry. This program element indicates that the work-based learning experiences you receive (paid-work experiences, job shadowing etc.) go hand-in-hand with what you are learning through your courses.

### #6

## ALTERNATIVE SECONDARY SCHOOL SERVICES OR DROPOUT RECOVERY SERVICES

WIOA Youth programs are designed to help develop you into a leader. Leadership activities may include community and service learning projects, peer mentoring and tutoring, training in decision making and problem solving scenarios, and life skills training, including parenting and work behavior training.

## #7

## SUPPORTIVE SERVICES

Gas cards, Uber and Lyft rides, new tires for your car, help paying your phone bill, child care assistance, help paying your rent or mortgage, and payments for employment related expenses including job interview attire are just some of the many supportive services provided by WIOA Youth programs. This form of assistance is meant to remove barriers in your life that may affect your ability to complete your credential or find a job. When you participate in a WIOA Youth program, you have access to a supportive service budget of $1,200 per calendar year.

**EXAMPLES OF SUPPORTIVE SERVICES EXPENSES**

- ✔ Gas Cards
- ✔ Housing/Rental Costs
- ✔ Child Care/Dependent Care
- ✔ Job Interview Attire
- ✔ Medical & Perscription Fees
- ✔ Ridesharing Expenses
- ✔ Utility Bills
- ✔ Car Repairs
- ✔ Legal Fees
- ✔ Cell Phones

# #8

## ADULT MENTORING

Mentoring is an important component of WIOA Youth programs. You have the opportunity to establish a formal relationship with a professional who can offer guidance, support, and encouragement throughout your journey as a student and job-seeker. Mentors can be faculty, staff, or employees at a company. Mentoring assignments normally last at least 12 months.

#9

## FOLLOW-UP SERVICES

---

Another benefit of WIOA Youth programs is that you have access to services and resources even after you exit the program. Follow-Up services provide additional support to ensure you successfully transition into an employment opportunity or additional college training opportunities. Follow-Up services begin immediately after you earn your credential, complete your work experience, or exit the program for other reasons. Services provided during follow-up include supportive services, mentoring, financial literacy, resume and job assistance, and more. Follow-up services normally last 12 months.

# #10

## COMPREHENSIVE GUIDANCE AND COUNSELING

Mental health counseling, drug and alcohol abuse counseling, and other forms of guidance counseling are provided to individuals as needed. WIOA Youth programs can provide recommendations and referrals to free partner programs, or cover the cost of a counselor to have individual sessions with you.

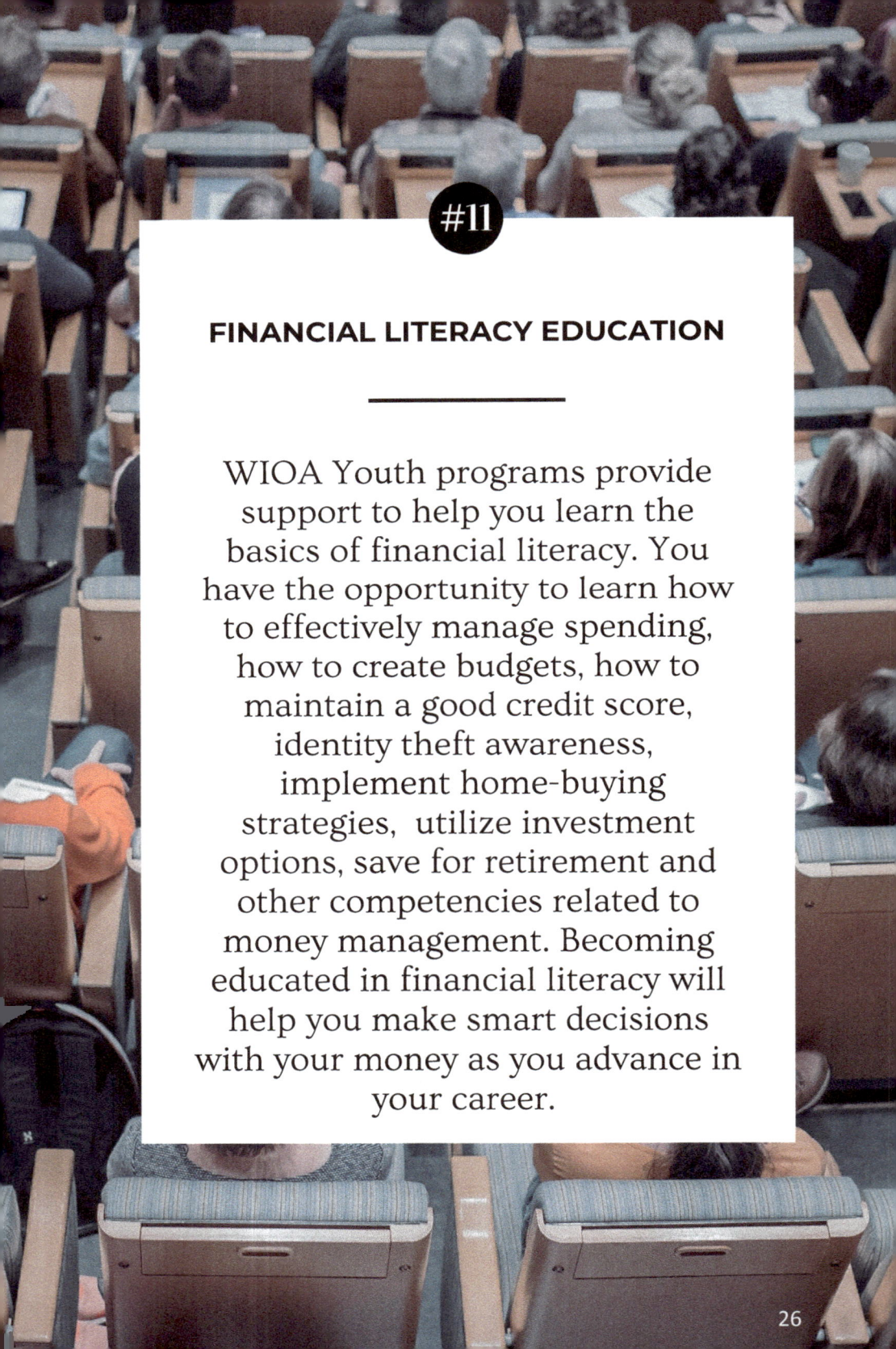

# #11

## FINANCIAL LITERACY EDUCATION

WIOA Youth programs provide support to help you learn the basics of financial literacy. You have the opportunity to learn how to effectively manage spending, how to create budgets, how to maintain a good credit score, identity theft awareness, implement home-buying strategies, utilize investment options, save for retirement and other competencies related to money management. Becoming educated in financial literacy will help you make smart decisions with your money as you advance in your career.

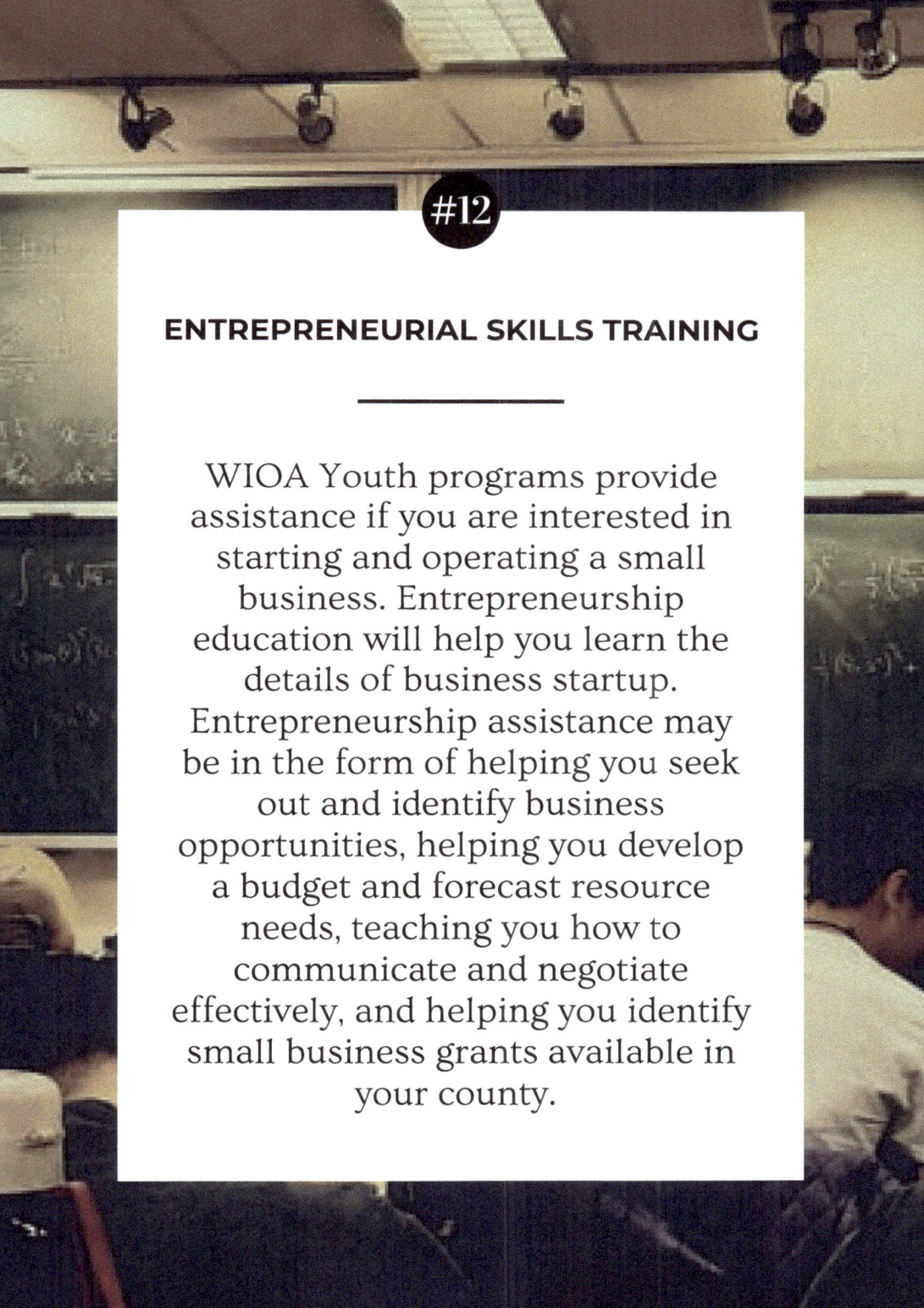

# #12

## ENTREPRENEURIAL SKILLS TRAINING

WIOA Youth programs provide assistance if you are interested in starting and operating a small business. Entrepreneurship education will help you learn the details of business startup. Entrepreneurship assistance may be in the form of helping you seek out and identify business opportunities, helping you develop a budget and forecast resource needs, teaching you how to communicate and negotiate effectively, and helping you identify small business grants available in your county.

## #13

## SERVICES THAT PROVIDE LABOR MARKET INFORMATION

It is important to understand the benefits and challenges of your job industry, how much money you can make in certain positions, and the education/training you will need to secure employment in the job of your choice. Labor market information is provided to you to help you make the appropriate decision about your career. WIOA Youth programs will help you calculate your potential earnings in the industry, help you identify challenges that may prevent you from being successful in your career, and equip you with the tools to ensure you are aware of the competencies required to thrive in your industry.

#14

## POST-SECONDARY PREPARATION AND TRANSITION ACTIVITIES

WIOA Youth programs can even provide assistance if you are currently in high school and preparing to transfer to a college or university. WIOA Youth programs provide SAT/ACT preparation assistance, help searching and applying for scholarships and grants, and help completing Financial Aid applications.

# CHAPTER TWO:
# WHO'S ELIGIBLE
## FOR A WIOA YOUTH PROGRAM?

# PRELIMINARY ELIGIBILITY CRITERIA

### CITIZENSHIP/ELIGIBLE TO WORK

To qualify for a WIOA Youth program, you must be a citizen of the United States, a lawfully admitted permanent resident alien, a refugee, an asylee, a parolee, or other immigrant status authorized by the Attorney General to work in the United States.

### SELECTIVE SERVICE/MILITARY STATUS

To be eligible for a WIOA Youth program, you must be in compliance with the Selective Service Act requirements stating that all males (citizens or non-citizens) living in the United States, who are at least 18 years old and born after December 31, 1959 and who are not in the armed services on active duty, must be registered.

### AGE AND SCHOOL STATUS

To qualify for a WIOA Youth (out-of-school) program, you must be 16-24 years old at the time of enrollment, not attending high school, and not enrolled in college credit courses.

# WIOA YOUTH QUALIFIERS

In addition to the preliminary eligibility criteria, potential candidates of WIOA Youth programs must meet at least one of the following qualifiers:

## AN INDIVIDUAL WHO DROPPED OUT OR DID NOT COMPLETE HIGH SCHOOL

This is defined as an individual who is no longer attending any form of school, and has not received a secondary school diploma or its recognized equivalent.

## AN INDIVIDUAL WITH A DISABILITY

This is defined as a physical or mental impairment that limits one or more major life activities. Documentation may include a record of the impairment, a copy of an Individual Education Plan or 504 Plan, a letter from a physician, or any other official documentation describing the disability.

## A LOW-INCOME INDIVIDUAL

This is defined as an individual who receives, or in the past six months has received, assistance through the Supplemental Nutrition Assistance Program (SNAP). This can also be a member of a family that is receiving, or in the past six months has received, SNAP benefits. A low income individual is also defined as someone who receives free or reduced lunch, a person living in a high poverty area, or a person in a family where the total family income does not exceed the poverty line.

# WIOA YOUTH QUALIFIERS

## AN INDIVIDUAL WHO HAS BEEN SUBJECT TO THE JUSTICE SYSTEM

This is defined as an individual who has been subject to the juvenile or adult justice system, and who requires assistance in overcoming barriers to employment as a result of the arrest or conviction.

## AN INDIVIDUAL WHO IS HOMELESS

This is defined as an individual who does not have permanent housing, who is living somewhere temporarily, or who lacks a fixed, regular, or adequate nighttime residence.

## AN INDIVIDUAL WHO IS PREGNANT OR PARENTING

This is defined as a mother, father, custodial or non-custodial parent. A pregnant individual can only be the expectant mother.

## AN INDIVIDUAL IN FOSTER CARE OR WHO HAS AGED OUT OF FOSTER CARE

This is defined as an individual who is currently in foster care, or an individual who was formerly in foster care but may have returned to their family before turning 18.

# ASSESSING YOUR MATH AND READING LEVELS

An assessment of your math and reading levels is required to enter a WIOA Youth program. There is no pass/fail result for the assessment; it is to measure where you are academically so the program can provide you with customized services and support.

# Common Documents Needed to Verify Your Eligibility

- ☑ Birth Certificate
- ☑ Driver's License
- ☑ State ID
- ☑ High School Diploma
- ☑ Social Security Card
- ☑ Public Assistance Records
- ☑ IEP, 504 Plan, or Disability Verification
- ☑ Transcripts

# CHAPTER THREE: HOW DO I APPLY

## FOR A WIOA YOUTH PROGRAM?

# DID YOU KNOW?

Every WIOA Youth program provider has case managers who assist you from the time you enter the program until one year after you exit. Case managers answer any questions you have, help you with the WIOA application and intake process, purchase books and supplies for your classes, provide you with gas cards, and much more!

# WIOA YOUTH APPLICATION PROCESS

**01 Find a WIOA Youth Provider**
There are WIOA Youth providers located in each state, and you are assigned a provider based on your residence.

**02 Review Available Career Programs**
Once you find your assigned WIOA Youth provider you can review the available program options that align with your career goals.

**03 Contact Your WIOA Youth Provider**
After reviewing available program options, you can contact your WIOA Youth provider to verify your eligibility and begin the intake process (completing a WIOA applications, submitting documents, etc.).

**04 Enter the WIOA Youth Program**
Once documents are submitted, and any additional requirements are met, you can now enter the WIOA Youth program.

## Reminder

You are becoming a role model for your family, friends, and peers. Your actions will become an example for others to follow. Make smart decisions.

Okay

# WHERE CAN I FIND WIOA YOUTH PROGRAM PROVIDERS?

WIOA Youth providers are located in every state nationwide. To find the provider closest to you, visit the website below or scan the QR code:

https://www.careeronestop.org/LocalHelp/EmploymentAndTraining/find-WIOA-training-programs.aspx?location=IL&persist=false

Scan the QR code to get started!

After you scan the code, select your state to find WIOA providers in your area.

# WHAT CAREER PROGRAM OR MAJOR CAN I CHOOSE?

There are hundreds of WIOA-approved programs/majors to choose from, and options available in every state. Every option you choose leads to an industry-recognized credential. This means that after completion of the program, you earn a credential (certificate, associate's degree, bachelor's degree, etc.) that gives you access to high-demand job opportunities. To find out what programs are available, visit the WIOA Youth provider's website, or ask a WIOA Youth staff member for a list of available programs in your area.

# SAMPLE CAREER PROGRAMS

Program availability may vary depending on your residence. Each state and county prioritizes specific programs depending on the occupational demand within the respective region.

ACCOUNTING
ADDICTIONS COUNSELING
ADMINISTRATIVE ASSISTANT
AUDIO PRODUCTION TECHNOLOGY
AUTOMOTIVE BODY REPAIR
AUTOMOTIVE TECHNOLOGY

BUSINESS
CONSTRUCTION
COMPUTER INFORMATION SYSTEMS
CRIMINAL JUSTICE
CULINARY ARTS
CYBERSECURITY

DENTAL ASSISTANT
ELECTRONICS TECHNOLOGY
EMERGENCY MEDICAL TECHNICIAN
ENGINEERING
FIRE SCIENCE TECHNOLOGY
FORKLIFT TRAINING

HEATING, VENTILATION, AND A/C
HOME INSPECTION
HUMAN RESOURCES MANAGEMENT
HUMAN SERVICES
INFORMATION TECHNOLOGY
MANUFACTURING

MARKETING
MEDICAL ASSISTANT
MEDICAL BILLING AND CODING
NURSE ASSISTANT
NURSING
OFFICE SOFTWARE SPECIALIST

PHARMACY TECHNICIAN
PHLEBOTOMY
PROJECT MANAGEMENT
TRUCK DRIVER TRAINING
WEBSITE DEVELOPMENT
WELDING

Developing productive habits can make achieving your goals easier and set you up for success in a WIOA Youth Program.

# CHAPTER FOUR:
# HOW DO I FIND BALANCE
## IN A WIOA YOUTH PROGRAM?

# BREAK YOUR LONG-TERM GOAL
## INTO SMALL DAILY ACTIONS

---

### 5-YEAR GOAL
What is a big goal you want to accomplish within the next five years?

### 1-YEAR GOAL
What is one action you can take this year toward your goal?

### MONTHLY GOAL
What is one action you can take this month toward your goal?

### WEEKLY GOAL
What is one action you can take this week toward your goal?

### DAILY GOAL
What is one action you can take today toward your goal?

### RIGHT NOW
What is one action you can take right now toward your goal?

# ESTABLISH A DAILY ROUTINE

A ROUTINE IS A SET OF ACTIONS AND HABITS YOU PERFORM ON A REGULAR BASIS TO HELP YOU STAY ORGANIZED. ROUTINES PROVIDE STRUCTURE TO YOUR DAY AND ALLOW YOU TO CONTROL WHAT YOU GET DONE. HAVING A ROUTINE HELPS YOU REMOVE DISTRACTIONS FROM YOUR LIFE, AND HELPS YOU MAKE CONSISTENT PROGRESS TOWARD YOUR GOALS.

**HERE ARE A FEW HABITS TO BUILD YOUR ROUTINE:**

| | |
|---|---|
| JOURNAL | TAKE A NAP |
| CREATE A TO-DO LIST | SCHEDULE YOUR DAY |
| GO FOR A WALK | COMPLETE YOUR TOP PRIORITY |
| EAT A HEALTHY SNACK | LEARN SOMETHING NEW |
| SPEND TIME WITH SOMEONE YOU LOVE | LISTEN TO MUSIC |
| EXERCISE/STRETCH | MAKE YOUR BED |
| READ | PRACTICE SELF-CARE |
| WORK ON HOMEWORK | REVIEW YOUR GOALS |
| SET TIME LIMITS FOR CERTAIN ACTIVITIES | WORK ON A SIDE HUSTLE |
| REFLECT ON YOUR ACCOMPLISHMENTS | PREPARE FOR THE NEXT DAY |
| WATCH SOMETHING INFORMATIVE | VISIT A FRIEND |

# Tips on Getting Organized

Develop a daily routine and stick to it.

Use a planner or calendar for keeping track of your appointments.

Declutter your workspace at least once a week.

Create your own deadlines before the actual due dates for assignments to give yourself time to review your work and make changes if needed.

Keep one notebook or binder for each subject.

# Tips on Getting Organized

Designate a specific study space and study time each day or week.

Use sticky notes to help yourself remember things.

Take five minutes each evening to plan your next day.

Break down big tasks into smaller tasks.

Pick out your outfit the day before.

# GET AN ACCOUNTABILITY PARTNER

---

An accountability partner is a person who helps you make consistent progress toward your goals. They help you stay focused on what is important to you, and encourage you to stay on track until your goals are complete. An accountability partner also helps you avoid distractions and activities that have nothing to do with your goals. An accountability partner can assist you with studying for a big exam, help you make progress toward a paper you need to write, or simply encourage you to stay positive and productive when you need motivation.

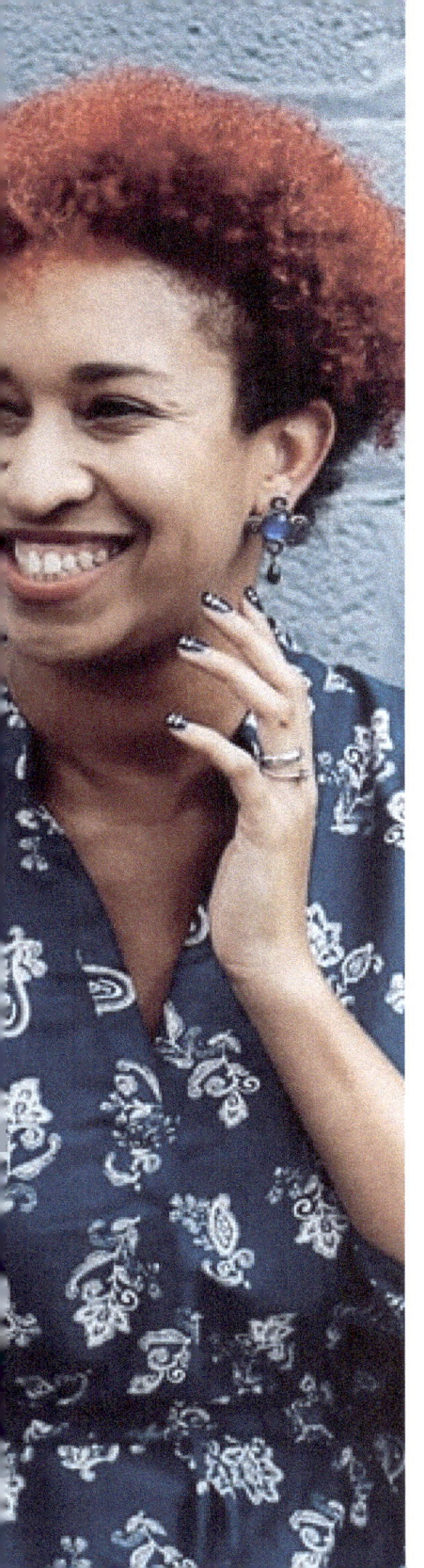

# 4 Tips for Choosing an Accountability Partner

**1** Choose someone you trust and someone who can help you make progress toward your goals and tasks.

**2** Talk to your accountability partner about your goals and why you want to accomplish them.

**3** Discuss with your accountability partner what action you need to take to accomplish your goals.

**4** Schedule regular check-ins with your accountability partner to ensure you make progress toward your goals.

*A WIOA Youth case manager can act as an accountability partner that will help you develop a plan and set goals within the program.*

# RECORD YOUR CLASS LECTURES

Sometimes, information presented in class can be complex and difficult to understand. Lectures can be fast-paced and very in-depth. To avoid feeling overwhelmed with note-taking, consider recording your lectures. Recording your class lectures ensures you don't miss anything, and having a recording allows you to easily refer back to the audio, or video, for studying purposes.

# Take a Social Media Break

Social media is a great way to stay in contact with family, friends, co-workers and peers, but spending too much time on social media also prevents you from being productive. It is important to always have a balance, and that is why taking a social media break is vital to ensuring you are completing your academic and career goals. Here are a few tips for setting social media boundaries for yourself.

## Tips for Taking a Social Media Break

- Set limits by tracking your social media time.
- Turn off notifications for certain time periods.
- Delete social media apps from your phone when you are taking a longer break.
- Schedule "social media time" to commit to only going on social media during certain times of the day.
- Put your phone down and out of reach when you are taking shorter breaks.
- Tell a friend (or accountability partner) you are taking a break from social media so they can help hold you accountable.

# UNDERSTAND YOUR LEARNING STYLE

## AUDITORY

Auditory learners receive information best through hearing. Speeches, presentations, lectures, verbal lessons, discussions, podcasts, and audiobooks are ways auditory learners retain information.

## VISUAL

Visual learners receive information best through seeing. Charts, grids photos, videos, posters, mind maps, timelines, and forms of color coding helps visual learners retain information.

## KINESTHETIC

Kinesthetic learners receive information from feeling, touching, and hands-on activities. Field trips, games, demonstrations, experiments, arts and crafts, group work, and body movements are ways kinesthetic learners retain information.

# Use Multiple Colors When Taking Notes

No matter what your learning style is, color-coding your notes can help you organize information more effectively, and study more efficiently. Color-coding involves using specific colors to highlight certain themes within your notes. Color-coding allows you to rapidly find information within your notes without having to review each page word-for-word. You can use a pen or a highlighter to color-code your notes, just remember to color-code right after your initial note-taking session so you can easily refer back to them later.

# Break Your Long-Term Assignments Into Small Chunks

**1.** Write down the due date of each project, paper, quiz, and exam (on a calendar, in a planner, or somewhere visible).

**2.** Assign your own deadline (at least a few days in advance of the actual due date) to complete the task. This gives you time to review before submitting.

**3.** Set reminders in your phone for each due date and deadline.

**4.** Gather all resources and materials needed for each task.

**5.** Spend time working on one task, one day at a time. ONLY focus on one task each day.

**6.** Repeat until each task is completed.

**7.** Review your work and prepare to submit.

# REWARD YOURSELF
## FOR MAKING PROGRESS

REWARDING YOURSELF IS A WAY TO ENCOURAGE AND MOTIVATE YOURSELF TO KEEP MAKING PROGRESS TOWARD YOUR GOALS. WHEN YOU FINISH A TASK OR A PROJECT, REWARD YOURSELF WITH SOMETHING YOU ENJOY LIKE WATCHING A FAVORITE MOVIE, EATING YOUR FAVORITE MEAL, DOING SOMETHING FUN WITH FRIENDS, OR TAKING PERSONAL TIME TO DO SOMETHING RELAXING. ALTHOUGH IT IS IMPORTANT TO WORK HARD TO COMPLETE WORK YOU HAVE TO DO, IT IS EQUALLY IMPORTANT TO CELEBRATE YOUR PROGRESS. ANY SMALL STEP TOWARD ACHIEVING YOUR GOALS IS WORTH ACKNOWLEDGING.

**Message**     NOW

Never limit the vision you have for yourself based on where you are right now. Dream big and aim for the stars, but remember to take things one step at a time.

# DON'T TAKE ON TOO MANY THINGS AT ONCE

One of the biggest mistakes made in WIOA Youth programs is taking on too many activities at once. Overcommitting leads to feeling overwhelmed. Take things slow. Start by taking one or two classes at a time to get adjusted to the new responsibilities of being a student and balancing everything else on your plate. Once you feel comfortable, you can increase your activities. It may take a little longer to complete the program but by taking things slow you will be less stressed and more productive.

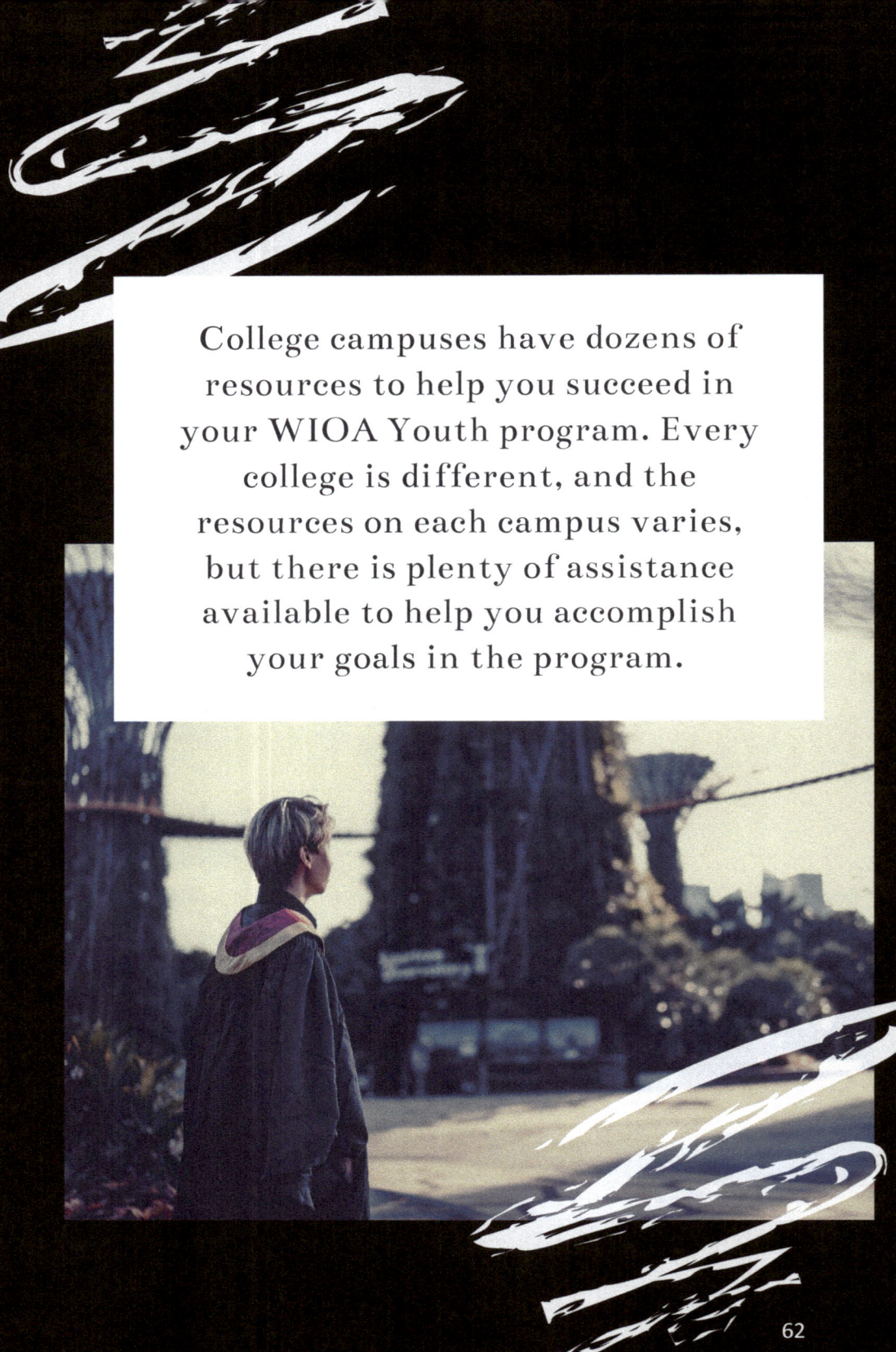

College campuses have dozens of resources to help you succeed in your WIOA Youth program. Every college is different, and the resources on each campus varies, but there is plenty of assistance available to help you accomplish your goals in the program.

# CHAPTER FIVE:
# WHAT ACADEMIC RESOURCES CAN HELP ME SUCCEED IN A WIOA YOUTH PROGRAM?

# TOUR THE CAMPUS BEFORE CLASSES START

It is important to become familiar with the campus before you begin classes. Learn where your classes are and how long it will take to get to each room. Become familiar with parking, restrooms, cafeterias, computer labs, and other locations on campus. Touring the campus will allow you to feel more comfortable when you are navigating on the first day of classes.

# Attend an Orientation Session

An orientation is another way to become familiar with your college campus, the services offered to students, and what to expect when you arrive on campus. During an orientation, you learn about activities and student organizations, athletic teams and intramurals, and the various departments at the college that can be a resource to you. Many colleges offer orientations in-person and online to provide flexibility. To find out what orientations may be offered, contact your Admissions department.

# USE AN ADVISOR TO HELP YOU SELECT COURSES

Advisors are individuals who help you choose courses, register for courses, improve your grades, and much more. They monitor your academic performance to ensure you fulfill all of your graduation requirements. Advisors can help connect you to valuable resources on campus, and refer you to organizations that can assist you off-campus.

---

## VISIT AN ADVISOR IF YOU:

- Have questions about choosing a major.
- Want to map out your courses for the next semester.
- Have questions about adding/dropping a course.
- Need help navigating campus and finding an exact location.
- Need help getting in contact with your instructor.
- Are struggling with a personal issue and can use some assistance.

Remember to visit your advisor frequently (at least one time each semester) and connect with your advisor when it's time for you to register for courses.

# Register for classes the day they open

It can be frustrating trying to get into a specific course just to find out that the course is filled up. It can be even more discouraging if the class you anticipated on taking is what prevents you from graduation, or completing your program of study on time. Registering for courses the day they open allows you to have first choice of course offerings. When you register early, you secure your seat in the class, and you won't have to request to be placed on a waitlist.

# APPLY FOR ADDITIONAL AID

In addition to WIOA funding, you may be eligible for other forms of financial assistance that you won't ever have to pay back. Colleges often have scholarships based on academic performance, athletic participation, gender, ethnicity, military status, your parents' place of employment, and many more categories. Some financial aid sources can even be used for costs unrelated to school such as living/housing expenses. To find out what you may qualify for, contact your financial aid department or scholarship office.

# TAKE A CLEP EXAM

The College Level Examination Program (CLEP) is a resource that allows you to earn college credits by taking an exam instead of earning your credits by enrolling in a course.

CLEP is a program that allows you to take an exam to earn anywhere between 1-12 college credits when you pass the exam. The credits you earn are used for introductory-level and general education courses and there are over 33 subjects to choose from including English, Sociology, Math, Psychology, History, Biology, Chemistry, and Humanities.

Most exams are multiple choice and taken on a computer. There is no set schedule for taking the exam so you can study and take it at your own pace. Each exam is around $87 dollars and takes 90-120 minutes to complete. This saves time and money compared to spending $300-$400 a credit hour for a 16-week course.

Discuss this option with your case manager to find out if it is the best option for you.

## Reminder

ALWAYS check your student email. Many schools use a student email account to communicate important information like registration, grade postings, and emergency updates. Checking your email multiple times a week ensures you receive all vital information.

_____

**Got it**

# BUILD STRONG RELATIONSHIPS WITH YOUR INSTRUCTORS

## WHY?

1. They can give you feedback to help you improve your grade.
2. They can serve as a mentor to you and give you advice on various topics.
3. They can offer information on scholarships, jobs, and other opportunities.
4. They can serve as a reference for future job interviews.
5. They can write letters or recommendation on your behalf.

## HOW?

1. Look them up online to learn about their professional accomplishments.
2. Introduce yourself.
3. Participate in class.
4. Visit them during their office hours.
5. Ask them for their perspective on how you can be a successful student.
6. Share your goals with them.
7. Keep in contact with them even after your class ends for the semester.

# USE THE WRITING CENTER TO HELP YOU WITH YOUR PAPERS

Adjusting to college-level writing can be tough. You may benefit from visiting a writing center to help you enhance your writing and editing skills. Writing centers are resources on most college campuses that help you with your papers, essays, research, and reports. Writing centers are staffed by tutors who can help you from the idea stage to the final version of your paper. Services are usually offered in-person and online, and you can visit as many times as you want.

# Use Your College's Free Tutoring Services

Most colleges have tutoring centers or tutoring services available to students for free. Tutoring centers are staffed by tutors who can help you clarify assignments, and work with you to understand concepts that your instructor presented in class. Tutors may also assist you with enhancing your time management and study skills, provide practice problems you may see on a future exam, and help you overcome difficulties you may have with your coursework. Tutors can help you in a variety of different subjects and you can usually visit as many times as you want.

# JOIN A STUDENT ORGANIZATION

Student organizations are groups of students on campus who meet regularly and have similar goals or interests. Student organizations are great ways to meet other students and build friendships. In a student organization, you may learn things like time management, organizational skills, teamwork, and collaboration. Joining a student organization looks great on your resume because it shows employers that you have a social side and that you can work well with peers. There are a variety of different student organizations to choose from. Categories range from academic, cultural, faith-based, honors, sports, gaming, community service, and much more.

# USE THE COLLEGE'S DISABILITY AND ACCOMMODATION SERVICES

All colleges have services available for students with disabilities, or students who require accommodations and learning resources. Disability services are designed to ensure access to education for all students with disabilities.

Accommodation services may include:

- EXTENDED TIME FOR TESTING IN A QUIET TEST ENVIRONMENT.
- HAVING A DESIGNATED NOTE-TAKER IN CLASS.
- MODIFIED OR ENLARGED CLASSROOM/READING MATERIALS.
- PREFERENTIAL CLASSROOM SEATING.
- DUE DATE EXTENSIONS FOR PROJECTS AND PAPERS.
- EXAM READERS AND TRANSCRIBERS.
- SCHOLARSHIPS FOR STUDENTS WITH DISABILITIES.

All information collected is confidential, and you normally work with a staff member who helps you coordinate your accommodations.

## USE THE COUNSELING CENTER TO STRENGTHEN YOUR MENTAL HEALTH

Many colleges offer counseling services to support students through mental health challenges, wellness barriers, trauma, stress, and other difficulties. Counseling services can be the resource you need to help you through a tough time, while also balancing your life responsibilities.

## COUNSELING AND THERAPY SERVICES MAY INCLUDE:

- One-on-one sessions with counselors.
- Mental health screenings.
- Help overcoming substance abuse.
- Help overcoming eating disorders.
- Referrals for additional help.
- Prevention programming.
- Mental health education.
- Workshops.
- Virtual and in-person sessions.

Contact your WIOA Youth provider to learn about additional services.

*This is a new transition for you. Things may seem unfamiliar, and even a little scary. Just remember, you're not going through this alone. WIOA Youth programs are designed to help you overcome obstacles like anxiety, depression, and even stress.*

# CHAPTER SIX:
# WHAT CAN I DO FOR MY MENTAL HEALTH IN A WIOA YOUTH PROGRAM?

# INCREASE YOUR SELF-AWARENESS

Self-awareness is your ability to understand your thoughts, feelings, beliefs, behaviors, and actions. Having self-awareness provides insight into who you are and how you react to situations. Self-awareness promotes emotional wellness, confidence, and self-esteem by giving you the ability to identify your strengths, and work to improve your weaknesses. You can increase your self-awareness by doing things like journaling, making a list of your strengths and weaknesses, and asking the people who know you best for feedback on what you can improve.

# EMBRACE FAILURE

YOU ARE EXPERIENCING A NEW JOURNEY. DO NOT BE SO HARD ON YOURSELF OR FEEL LIKE YOU HAVE TO UNDERSTAND HOW TO GET EVERYTHING RIGHT. EXPECT SETBACKS TO HAPPEN. THEY ARE NEEDED FOR YOU TO LEARN AND GROW. REMEMBER, FAILURE IS NECESSARY FOR SUCCESS.

# FORGIVE YOURSELF WHEN YOU MAKE MISTAKES.

You have messed up in the past and you will mess up again. Everyone makes mistakes, and every successful person has failed. You are no different. Never punish yourself for doing something wrong. Instead, take advantage of the opportunity to try again.

## Look at Obstacles as Opportunities

Challenges are a part of life. You have to learn to accept them, and appreciate the mistakes that give you knowledge and understanding of what to do in the future. Problems you face are not stop signs. They are opportunities to grow. Start replacing "Why is this happening to me?" with "What is this trying to teach me?" There is a hidden lesson to be learned from every difficulty you face.

# LEARN HOW TO SAY "NO"

BEING A STUDENT REQUIRES DEDICATION, AND LOTS OF PRIORITIZING. YOU HAVE TO BE SELECTIVE WITH HOW YOU SPEND YOUR TIME. IF YOU TRY TO DO EVERYTHING YOU WON'T BE ABLE TO GIVE 100% TO ANYTHING. SAY "NO" TO THE THINGS THAT ARE UNIMPORTANT, AND HAVE NOTHING TO DO WITH YOUR GOALS.

# RESPOND INSTEAD OF REACTING

It is normal for you to face stressful situations in college. There are many situations you will face that are simply out of your control. Remember, if you cannot control what is happening to you, control how you *respond* to what is happening to you. You are in complete control of how you respond to the stressful situations. Use your WIOA Youth resources. Connect with a WIOA Youth staff member who can help get you the support you need.

# DID YOU KNOW?

*WIOA YOUTH PROGRAMS COVER COUNSELING, THERAPY, MEDICINE, AND OTHER PHYSICAL AND MENTAL HEALTH EXPENSES? ASK A WIOA YOUTH STAFF MEMBER FOR DETAILS ON HOW TO RECEIVE FINANCIAL ASSISTANCE TO COVER THESE QUALIFYING EXPENSES.*

# Ask for Help

THERE ARE PEOPLE IN YOUR LIFE WHO HAVE EXPERIENCE OVERCOMING A CHALLENGE YOU MAY BE CURRENTLY FACING. ASKING FOR HELP IS THE MOST EFFICIENT WAY TO SOLVE A PROBLEM THAT MAY BE TOO DIFFICULT TO HANDLE ON YOUR OWN. ASKING FOR HELP CAN SOMETIMES BE DIFFICULT, AND EVEN SCARY. YOU MAY EVEN FEEL ASHAMED TO ASK FOR HELP, BUT REMEMBER, EVERYONE HAS RECEIVED (OR WILL RECEIVE) HELP AT SOME POINT IN LIFE. IT'S NOTHING TO FEEL EMBARRASSED ABOUT. ASKING FOR HELP SAVES YOU TIME, DECREASES STRESS, AND ALLOWS YOU TO DEVELOP RELATIONSHIPS WITH GREAT INDIVIDUALS WHO KNOW HOW TO SOLVE PROBLEMS.

_____

# Step Outside of Your Comfort Zone

DO NOT ALLOW THE NEGATIVE THINGS THAT HAPPENED TO YOU PREVENT YOU FROM THE GREAT OPPORTUNITIES THAT ARE WAITING FOR YOU. IT IS NORMAL TO FEEL NERVOUS ABOUT STEPPING OUTSIDE OF YOUR COMFORT ZONE, BUT THE MORE OPEN YOU ARE TO EXPERIENCING NEW THINGS, THE MORE CONFIDENT YOU WILL BECOME IN YOUR ABILITY TO FACE NEW SITUATIONS. PUSHING YOURSELF TO TRY SOMETHING NEW WILL HELP YOU GROW AND DEVELOP INTO A STRONGER PERSON.

# Evaluate Your Relationships

Who are the people you spend time with the most?

   Do you share similar interests?

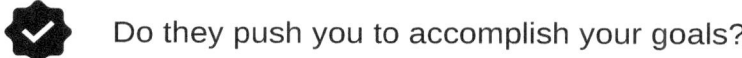   Do they push you to accomplish your goals?

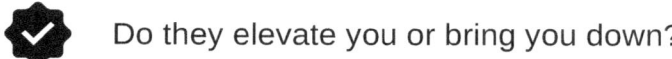   Do they elevate you or bring you down?

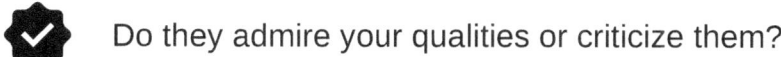   Do they admire your qualities or criticize them?

   Are they motivators or energy drainers?

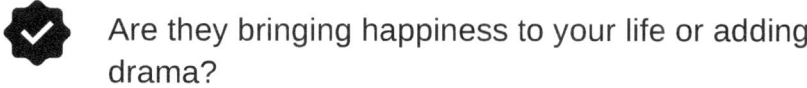   Are they bringing happiness to your life or adding drama?

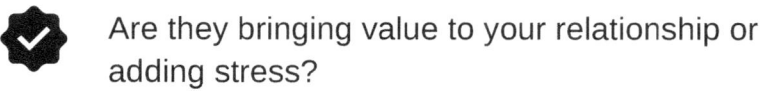   Are they bringing value to your relationship or adding stress?

Evaluating your relationships helps you determine who to keep in your inner circle and who to keep at a distance.

WIOA Youth programs provide career development and personal branding assistance to help you secure a job in your desired career industry. Paid-work experiences, job shadowing, on-the-job training, and mentoring are just a few ways the program can help accelerate your career.

# CHAPTER SEVEN:
# HOW CAN A WIOA YOUTH PROGRAM PREPARE ME FOR MY CAREER?

# EXPLORE CAREER OPTIONS

Career exploration is researching, learning, understanding, and evaluating the various career paths you can pursue in life. Through career exploration, you become familiar with different job industries and employment opportunities. Career exploration removes career frustration and uncertainty by guiding you through your employment options, and helping you make the best job choice for your future. Through career exploration, you also learn things like how much education is needed to enter a specific career field, starting salary information, industry trends and challenges, and opportunities available to get promoted within your industry.

To begin exploring, first **RESEARCH** a set of careers and industries to learn about the work performed in those respective industries. Next, **EVALUATE** positions that interest you within the industries you have identified. Look at job descriptions, review LinkedIn profiles, and identify any other resources to help you understand the professional opportunities available. Then, **DISCUSS** the careers and positions you have researched with a WIOA Youth staff member. Communicate why you have an interest in the careers, and how they would be a good fit for you. Finally, **DECIDE** on a career training program (or major) that is a direct path to the career industry you have selected.

# Participate in a Job Shadowing Opportunity

Job shadowing is a unique and simple opportunity that allows you to learn about positions within a specific job industry.

In a job shadowing opportunity, you follow a professional in their work environment to gain an understanding of job responsibilities, workplace culture, and skills needed.

Job shadowing can last an hour, multiple hours, a week, or longer. You and the person you will be job shadowing will agree on the duration.

Job shadowing also helps you develop professional relationships that can be beneficial to you when you are looking for your future job.

When job shadowing, you get to ask the person you are shadowing detailed questions that can help you confirm whether or not the industry or position is the right fit for you.

To get started, contact a WIOA Youth staff member to learn about the job shadowing opportunities available.

# PARTICIPATE IN A PAID-WORK EXPERIENCE

One of the greatest challenges students face after graduation is finding a job in their career field that pays well. Employers want you to have a degree or certificate that shows you are competent in your desired career industry, but they also want you to have experience, knowledge, and skills prior to applying for the job in your industry. It is frustrating to apply for a job, only to find out that you do not have enough relevant experience to get hired. Participating in a paid-work experience is your solution to ensure you get hired for competitive career opportunities.

WIOA Youth programs offer 8-12 week paid-work experiences that allow you to gain career-related skills that would otherwise be difficult to obtain on your own. Paid-work experiences are flexible, convenient, and require no extensive skillset to get started. You have the option of participating in a paid-work experience before started classes, or you can choose to do a paid-work experience without taking classes at all. Talk to a WIOA Youth staff member to find out what paid-work experiences are available in your area.

# PARTICIPATE IN ON-THE-JOB TRAINING

On-the-job training (OJT) is a program under WIOA that allows employers to hire and train you while getting reimbursed up to 50% of training and wage expenses. The goal of OJT is to help you develop skills that lead to high-wage employment opportunities.

ASK A WIOA YOUTH STAFF MEMBER ABOUT ON-THE-JOB TRAINING

### Here is how OJT works:

First, you let a WIOA Youth staff member know that you are interested in OJT. A WIOA Youth staff member will then help you get hired with an employer that aligns with your career goals. The employer is reimbursed up to 50% of the wages they pay you (along with any qualifying training expenses). In exchange, the employer provides training, coaching, and additional supervision necessary for you to be successful in your job. OJT can be just what you need to gain work experience, skills, and a great paying job.

## USE INFORMATIONAL INTERVIEWS TO BUILD PROFESSIONAL RELATIONSHIPS

Conducting an informational interview is a way to develop relationships with professionals to learn about their specific job or job industry. Informational interviews are brief interactions you make with professionals where you have the opportunity to ask them a series of questions about their career field.

The benefit of an informational interview is that you are given a safe environment to ask questions that could help propel your career in the right direction. You may already know all about a specific job industry but speaking to someone who actually works in the field gives you the opportunity to get the day-to-day details about how a career in that industry looks.

Another benefit of conducting an informational interview is that it provides you with visibility—giving you a way to stand out in a hidden job market by connecting you with professionals in your desired career field. This could give you access to numerous career opportunities; like learning about a job opening through an informational interview before the job even gets posted

Remember, the people you are interviewing are doing you a favor, so work around what is convenient for their schedule and remember to remain respectful of their time.

Limit your interview to 15-30 minutes based on how the conversation is going.

Informational interviews are about getting information about your career industry, not about getting a job. Although, the relationship could lead to a job opportunity. Do your research on the industry before the interview so that you can have a set agenda for the conversation. Remember to follow up by sending a thank you email within 24 hours after the informational interview.

**Steps to take for an informational interview:**

1  Start by making a list of job titles you would potentially apply for in the future.

2. Review job descriptions for each job title to confirm that you may be interested in the specific job.

3.  Identify three professionals within your desired job industry to potentially interview. Try to find professionals who have at least three to five years of experience in the industry. You can also try to find individuals that are holding (or previously held) positions that you seek to hold in the future.

4. Do you know anyone who can introduce you to any of the professionals? If so, ask to be introduced. Otherwise, proceed by sending an introduction email or a message through LinkedIn.

# Informational Interview Template

*Hello Ms./Mr. _____*

*I recently found your LinkedIn profile while reviewing careers in the field of _____. I see that you _____ (reference their position title or a few professional details you found on them). I am interested in pursuing a career as a _____ in the future and I could really use your advice on how to be successful in the _____ industry. Do you have time in the next two weeks to share any tips or strategies you've learned in your career? I am flexible and can speak in person, over the phone, or via video. Thank you for your time and have a great day.*

Keep your message very brief. It may be a very busy time for the person you are reaching out to so do not expect an immediate response. If you have any connections with the person you are reaching out to, mention those connections in the email. You can also mention the connections in the subject line (ex: Brian Peck suggested that we connect).

Remember to be formal with the first email and let the tone of the person's response dictate your future style of communication. Once they respond, mention general time windows ("I am free Mondays, Wednesdays and Fridays after 11am) but leave the schedule decision up to them.

## Questions to Ask During the Informational Interview

- How did you get started in this industry?
- What experiences best prepared you for your job?
- Were you formally trained for this position?
- What education is necessary in order to be successful in this field?
- What experiences or skills are necessary in order to be successful in this field?
- What are some of the biggest challenges facing your company and your industry today?
- What does a typical career path look like in your industry?
- What is unique about your company compared to other companies?
- What do you like most/least about your career?
- What are employers looking for from candidates in this industry?
- What advice do you have for me right now in my current position?
- What do you wish you knew starting out that you know now about your career?

## WORK WITH A MENTOR

Find someone who is successfully doing what you want to do and build a relationship with that person. Call them, take them out to lunch, and find out what they did to reach their success. Then follow similar strategies they used to become a better version of yourself.

## WHY WORK WITH A MENTOR?

- Mentors help you develop personal and professional skills that help you in life.
- Mentors help you access career opportunities that may be difficult to get on your own.
- Mentors provide guidance on how you can gain new skills and experiences.
- Mentors help to increase your confidence.
- Mentors provide continuous constructive feedback on areas you can improve.
- Mentors provide support and a safe space to share ideas and address concerns.

## TIPS FOR WORKING WITH A MENTOR

- Find someone who has done what you want to do in the future. Holding an informational interview is a great way to find a mentor.
- Be open to learning, sharing feedback and receiving feedback.
- Show appreciation for the time your mentor invests in you.
- Schedule bi-weekly or monthly chats with your mentor, and set clear expectations on what you want to achieve.

# Create an Elevator Pitch

An elevator pitch is an introduction that is used to communicate a professional message about yourself. It is your own commercial that showcases who you are, what skills you have, and how you make an impact. Elevator pitches are usually 30-60 seconds, but impressive enough to capture the listener's attention, leaving them wanting to know more about you.

## 01

The Introduction: First, start with a quick introduction about yourself. This includes your name, your background and what it is that you actually do. This is a great time to talk about your job title and job industry. Include your major and your anticipated graduation date if you are pursuing a credential. If you have graduated, include the school you attended and the title of your degree.

## 02

The Problem: Next, talk about your experience. The most effective way to do this is to introduce a set of problems you have encountered in your career. Every job industry has obstacles, and speaking about these obstacles shows the listener that your analytical skills have allowed you to clearly identify problems in the past.

## 03

The Solution: After you introduce a challenge that you have faced in the past, talk about your experience overcoming the challenge. Your goal is to help the listener understand that you are a person that knows how to solve problems, and your track record proves this to be true.

## 04

The Wrap-Up: Finally, talk about what you bring to the table and what you can offer as a professional. This is the selling piece of your elevator pitch. This is where you relate your experiences, skills, and abilities to the specific needs of your career industry. What experience have you gone through that makes you stand out as a professional? How can you add value to your career industry? These are questions you can answer as you close your elevator pitch.

# TIPS FOR BUILDING RELATIONSHIPS

- ATTEND AN EVENT ON CAMPUS OR A SOCIAL EVENT THAT APPEALS TO YOUR INTEREST.
- INVITE A CLASSMATE OR CO-WORKER TO LUNCH OR TO GET COFFEE.
- REACH OUT TO LIKE-MINDED PEOPLE ON SOCIAL MEDIA.
- JOIN A SOCIAL GROUP FOR MEETING NEW PEOPLE.
- JOIN A STUDENT ORGANIZATION OR INTRAMURAL SPORTS TEAM.
- TAKE TIME TO UNPLUG FROM YOUR PHONE AND START A CONVERSATION WITH SOMEONE AROUND YOU.

# GOOGLE YOURSELF

One of the easiest things you can do for your personal brand is to Google yourself. Googling yourself gives you an opportunity to see what the public sees, and it allows you to take the necessary steps to remove information if it is damaging to your personal brand.

Start with a basic search for your name by entering it in the search bar. If you have a common name you might have to go through the first three pages in the search results to see what shows up. If you do not find anything in the search results add other characteristics like the city you live in, the name of your school, or the company you work for.

Next, search to see what photos of yourself you can find on Google by visiting images.google.com. If you identify yourself in any of the photos click on them to find out where they are being housed. Google also allows you to search by image. Simply click the camera icon and paste the link of the image in the search bar, or upload the image. Google will search the internet for that specific image whether your name is attached to it or not.

After searching through images, search for your past and current email addresses and phone numbers. These can be commonly attached to social media accounts, blogs, or other websites. Finally, do a Google search on your social media accounts and usernames. You might be surprised what shows up as public information that you thought was hidden.

# CREATE A RESUME

A resume is a formal document that allows you to showcase your experience, skills, and accomplishments to employers. Resumes are often needed to apply for jobs because it gives the employer an idea of what to expect if you were to be hired. Resumes also help you communicate your strengths, and the ways you stand out as a professional. Most importantly, resumes show the employer what impact you have made in your previous positions. When you search for a job, having a strong resume is vital.

## TIPS FOR CREATING AN IMPACTFUL RESUME

- Dedicate time to updating your resume before applying.
- Use bullet points.
- Use 10-12 point font.
- List accomplishments, not responsibilities.
- Start each bullet point with an action verb like "directed, facilitated, achieved, supervised, etc."
- List your most recent experiences first.
- Quantify your resume by adding numbers
- Show what problems you have solved.
- Remove fluff phrases like "self-starter," "attention to detail," "excellent team player," "motivated," etc.
- Do not repeat yourself.
- Update your contact information.
- List a professional email address.
- Do not include the phrase "References available upon request." It is not needed.

# BROWSE RESUME SAMPLES ON INDEED

Indeed is the largest job website in the world with over 250 million monthly users and 10 new job listings added every second. Indeed is free to job seekers, allowing you to search for jobs, create job alerts, and apply for jobs that fit your career goals. Indeed has a huge selection of resume samples from a variety of job industries and titles that users can browse freely. Each resume sample is based on the most contacted resumes on Indeed, and skills and certifications based on job industries and titles have been added to each resume. To find a sample resume, you can search by job title or view all sample resumes listed on Indeed.

# Linked in

## MAKE A LINKEDIN PROFILE

LinkedIn is the largest professional social networking site in the world. It is a great way to build your personal brand, connect with employers and professionals in your industry, create a visual portfolio of your work, and access information and opportunities. LinkedIn allows you to showcase classes you take, honors and awards you earn, projects you complete, and other accomplishments. Millions of students use LinkedIn to find internships and job opportunities in college and beyond. It's free to use and easy to set up.

**VISIT WWW.LINKEDIN.COM TO GET STARTED.**

# ATTEND AT LEAST ONE CAREER FAIR EACH YEAR

A career fair is an event that gives employers the opportunity to promote jobs, internships, and other career opportunities to students and job-seekers. Career fairs are a chance to present yourself and articulate your strengths to employers. It is also a great way to build professional relationships, get career feedback and advice from professionals in your industry, and set up career opportunities for your future. Attending at least one career fair each year will help you become comfortable holding a professional conversation with employers — a skill that you will use for the rest of your life.

# TIPS FOR A SUCCESSFUL JOB SEARCH

- ☑ Have an updated resume ready at all times.
- ☑ Check your email daily.
- ☑ Have an updated LinkedIn profile.
- ☑ Read each job description 3X before you apply.
- ☑ Have an updated cover letter.
- ☑ Schedule informational interviews.
- ☑ Network regularly.
- ☑ Understand the company's mission before you apply.
- ☑ Always send a "thank you" after interviewing.
- ☑ Apply, even if you are not a 100% match.
- ☑ Post your resume on job sites like Indeed.
- ☑ Look up company reviews from former employees.
- ☑ Calculate your commute time before applying.
- ☑ Keep a record of all jobs you apply for.
- ☑ Hangout with a funny friend
- ☑ Make tweaks to your resume as needed.
- ☑ Keep a positive and optimistic attitude.

# FOLLOW-UP SERVICES

After completing your goals in a WIOA Youth Program, it is time to enter the final step in the program—Follow Up. When Follow Up occurs, you are exited from the WIOA Youth program, but you still have access to certain services and resources. Gas cards, job interview attire, help with bills, and job search assistance are just a few services you can access while in Follow Up. You also have access to your case advisor who can help you and answer any questions you have as you enter the next phase of your life, which may include establishing a personal brand, gaining financial literacy, looking for jobs, and developing valuable life skills.

# CHAPTER EIGHT:
# WHAT'S NEXT AFTER COMPLETING A WIOA YOUTH PROGRAM?

# CREATE A BUDGET

In order to manage your money, you have to know how much is coming in, and how much is going out. Having a budget gives you 100% control of your money by allowing you to estimate your income and expenses over time. Having a budget helps you understand your relationship with money and it allows you to identify your spending habits. A common rule to successful budgeting is to always spend less than what you earn. This will help you save money, stay out of debt, and allow you to invest for your future. To get started, you can download one of the many budgeting apps to track your income and expenses from the convenience of your phone or mobile device.

# START A RAINY DAY FUND

A rainy day fund is a stash of money set aside to cover one-time expenses that fall outside of your normal budget. Rainy day funds are used to pay for things like broken appliances, minor car expenses, and unexpected bills. Rainy day funds help you cover unexpected expenses without having to borrow money and go into debt. It also prevents you from having to use money from your main checking account to cover unexpected expenses.

Your rainy day fund should be between $400 and $1,000 to cover out-of-budget expenses. To begin saving for your rainy day fund, start by putting $25 away each month until you reach $250. Then work toward reaching $400. Keep going until you reach $750, then aim for $1,000. When unplanned expenses occur, your mind will be at ease knowing you have funds to cover them.

# ELIMINATE DEBT

To become financially independent it is critical that you decrease the amount of debt you have. Anything owed to someone else is considered debt. It is common to owe money on credit card bills, student loans, and other accounts. It is also important to take action to eliminate your debts as soon as you have the opportunity to do so. Debt is the enemy of wealth. It causes stress, anger, fear, anxiety, and sometimes depression.

Debt destroys your credit score, takes away from your happiness, and robs you of your freedom. To establish financial peace, you must first take the proper action to eliminate as much debt as you possibly can. Choosing to pay off your debts now will lead to more financial opportunities in your future. Use the Snowball Method to get out of debt.

**WHAT IS THE SNOWBALL METHOD FOR ELIMINATING DEBT?**

The Snowball Method is a commonly used strategy for getting out of debt. You simply pay your smallest debts off first. Then, once the small debts are paid off, you take the money you were using to pay off the small debts and pay toward your larger debts until those are paid off as well. To use the Snowball Method strategy, list all of your debts from smallest to largest.

Make minimum payments toward your smallest debt until it is paid off. Use any extra money you have to make additional payments toward your smallest debt. When your smallest debt is gone, start making minimum payments toward your next debt until that one is paid off. Repeat these steps until your debt is paid in full. The Snowball Method is designed to help you change your behavior with money so you never go into overwhelming debt again. By doing this, you'll gain a sense of accomplishment and relief when you begin to see your debts disappear.

# Understand Your Credit Score

Your credit score is calculated by your payment history, your credit utilization (the amount of credit you are using), the various types of credit you use, how long you have had credit, and inquiries made on your credit report. Credit scores range from 300-850 points.

## CREDIT RATINGS

Excellent Credit: 750-850
Good Credit: 700-749
Fair Credit: 650-699
Poor Credit: 600-649
Bad Credit: Below 600

A healthy credit score gives you more buying and negotiating power. It improves your chances of getting approved for apartments, gives you access to home and car loans, helps you avoid having to pay security deposits, and creates more investment opportunities.

# TIPS FOR MAINTAINING GOOD CREDIT

**1** Request a free credit report using AnnualCreditReport.com.

**2** Pay your credit card accounts down and don't use more than 30% of your overall credit limit.

**3** Check your credit score frequently.

**4** Do not co-sign on loans or credit cards that you can't afford to pay by yourself.

**5** Keep your unused accounts open. Closing them decreases your credit score.

**6** Pay at least the minimum payment every month, and make multiple payments when you can.

# PLAN FOR RETIREMENT

Having savings stashed away for retirement is the ultimate wealth-building strategy. Retirement accounts allow you to invest money for the future, while reaping the tax benefits now. When it comes to retirement planning, time can be your greatest asset or your worst enemy. If you start early, time is on your side, and building wealth becomes easier. But if you wait until retirement is just a few years away it will become extremely difficult to catch up with saving, and you may be forced to live on a fixed income.

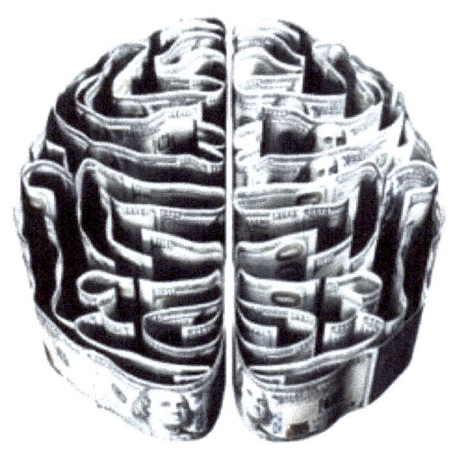

Although there are limits to the amount of money you can save each year, you are allowed to have more than one retirement account, setting you up for multiple streams of income for the future. Thanks to mobile apps and online resources, saving for retirement is now easier to do than ever before.

# NOTES

Congressional Research Service (2015). The Workforce Innovation and Opportunity Act and the One-Stop Delivery System. Retrieved on 10/4/19 from https://www.everycrsreport.com/files/20151027_R44252_0bf51008ea43db27d8e9436066f2b4a33feaa7e2.pdf.

Illinois Department of Commerce and Economic Opportunity (2019). WIOA approved training programs search. Retrieved on 10/5/19 from https://www.illinoisworknet.com/Training/Pages/WIOATrainingProgramSearch.aspx.

Jones, Tiffany & Berger, Katie (2018). A promise fulfilled: A framework for equitable free college programs. The Education Trust. Retrieved on 10/11/19 from https://s3-us-east-2.amazonaws.com/edtrustmain/wp-content/uploads/2018/09/05155636/A-Promise-Fulfilled-A-Framework-for-Equitable-Free-College-Programs-9.6-18.pdf.

Murphy, Joel and Murphy Shirley (2017). Get ready, get in, get through: factors that influence latino college student success, Journal of Latinos and Education. 17 (3-17), (2017).

Pitre, C, and Pitre, P. (2009). Increasing underrepresented high school students' college transitions and achievements. NASSP Bulletin, 93(2), 96-110.

Poutre, Alain, & Voight, Mamie (2018). The state of free college: Tennessee promise and New York's excelsior scholarship. Institute for Higher Education Policy. Retrieved on 10/15/2019 from http://www.ihep.org/research/publications/state-free-college-tennessee-promise-and-new-yorks-excelsior-scholarship.

Workforce GPS (2017). Retrieved on 10/6/2019 from: https://youth.workforcegps.org/resources/2017/03/09/11/34/WIOA-Youth-Program-Eligibility.

# ABOUT THE AUTHOR

**Marques J. Clark** is a researcher, grant writer, and former WIOA Youth program manager. Marques has a personal mission of removing hidden barriers to economic mobility, and he writes to educate audiences on topics related to education, employment, mental health and personal growth. Marques earned his Bachelor's of Arts in Sociology and his Master's of Science in Counseling and Higher Education from Northern Illinois University.

www.ingramcontent.com/pod-product-compliance
Lightning Source LLC
Chambersburg PA
CBHW040638100526
44583CB00038B/3068